MW00909339

KID'S VACATION DIARY

Have fun with
your own
travel diary
and activity book!

Plus: Travel games!
Pictures to draw! Things to do
for the best trip ever!

Other Marlor Press
Books for Kids:

**Kid's
Address
& Writing
Book**

KID'S VACATION DIARY

A fun diary and vacation book for use while traveling!

MARLOR PRESS, INC.

KID'S VACATION DIARY

Copyright 1991
MARLOR PRESS, INC.

Illustrations by Marlin Bree

Special thanks to all the kids, educators, parents & others
who contributed to this book, especially Bernice Gutzmer

ISBN 0-943400-23-6

First Printing: March, 1991.

Marlor Press books are distributed to the book trade by Contemporary Books Inc., Chicago, Ill

ML

MARLOR PRESS, INC.

4304 Brigadoon Drive/ Saint Paul, Minnesota/ 55126

Contents

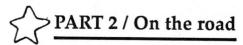

PART 1 / Getting ready for your trip

PART 2 / On the road

PART 3 / Memories

How to have fun with this book

 Congratulations! You're going on a trip.

This book can help make your vacation a lot more fun. It'll be your fun companion before and during your trip—for you to confide in, to write up your own adventures, and to spend many happy travel hours.

Your **Kid's Vacation Diary** is divided into three parts:

1/ Getting ready   2/ On the Road   3/ Memories

1/ Getting ready lets you do all sorts of interesting things before your vacation. Here you can make plans for what you want to see and do. With your parent's help, you can find out what you want to take along, make a list of things you want to do before you go, and jot down important information you want to keep with you.

2/ On the road is where you keep your *Daily Diary*. You can write down what you did today, what you liked best, what you saw that was funny, as well as some foods you ate. You can draw a picture. You'll also find fun travel games to play.

3/ Memories is where you can keep small souvenirs. Here's a fine place to paste in a ticket to a fun park, a picture, or a color post card you picked out.

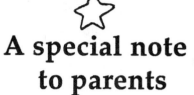 A special note to parents

This book is designed to make traveling more fun for children. It will also make it easier for them to travel with the family.

When children take an active part in preparing for a vacation or trip, they make an investment in the journey. With proper preparations, children can look forward to travel as fun and adventure. This book will help.

You can encourage your child to have a good outlook on travel by helping him or her prepare for the trip. Help her or him with the before-trip preparations such as the *Things I want to do before I go* section. Perhaps the child has a pet that needs to be boarded. Or a flower that needs caring for by a friend. Have him or her write these things down, and, when they are done, checked off.

One important part of your trip will be to get information about where you are going. You can get a book, magazine, or help the child write a letter to the local chamber of commerce or state tourism board (your local library has addresses). It will be exciting to have a packet of information come by mail, addressed to your child. Then, the child can learn about where you are going and even make a short list of what he or she wants to see and do on the trip. This lets the child anticipate the trip as a fun adventure.

A child can be involved in deciding what he or she wants to take along on the trip. After helping decide, he or she can help pack his or her own bag of clothing and supplies. You can make this a positive experience, for example, by your attitude and your words. The child will also find travel a lot more fun if there's lots to do. Favorite toys and games should be taken along, and the child should identify these in the *What I want to take along on my trip*. You can also help the child fill out *Important information I want to write down and take along* as well as the information in *People I want to send postcards to*.

You can also go over the *Today's Diary* pages with your child, helping him or her keep a record. You can encourage your child to write by making writing fun. Keep in mind that he or she will be quickly discouraged by criticism or even the suggestion that what they've done could be improved. If your child is too small to write, just ask the child to tell you what he or she wants to say. You don't have to be fancy, but your child will remember your love and your interest.

Travel games are a terrific way to beat the car-trip blues. Each day there is an entertaining game to pass the time. You can enter into this game and help have a great time. At the back of the book, there are more games for you and your child to enjoy.

Some older children enjoy having a little allowance of their own. On the diary pages, you can let them keep a record of what they spent, and their daily totals. This can help make the vacation special, too.

It's important to be very supportive of your child. Give him or her all your attention and encouragement and tell that you think what he or she has done is wonderful. And pretty soon, maybe it will be! Relax, and let your child have fun with this book. You will both have a better time on vacation.

Part One

Getting ready for your trip

⭐ Things I want to do before I go

⭐ What I want to see and do on my trip

⭐ Important information to take along

⭐ People I want to send cards to

⭐ What I want to take along

⭐ Special notes for my trip

☆ ☆ ☆
Getting ready for your trip

You can have as much fun getting ready as actually traveling. That's because there's so much to look forward to—and you can learn as you prepare for your trip.

Here are some things to do before you go:

- Get information on where you're going. You can look this up in books or magazines at the library. If you have time, you also can write for tourist information from the state or city you plan to visit. An adult can help.

- Write down what you want to see and do.

- Write down what you want to take along to play with and to wear.

- Find out what important information you want to take along and write that down. This includes emergency numbers and names.

- Write down the names and addresses of people you want to send cards to. Think of how pleased a friend, a grandparent, or an aunt will be when they get a special remembrance from you.

But above all, enjoy yourself! Dream a little as you prepare for your trip. You can have a wonderful time.

Things I want to do before I go

Before you leave, there are some things you will want to do to get ready for your trip. You will want to learn more about where you are going, think about what you want to take along, and, in general, be helpful as you begin your vacation adventure. Below, just list what you *want* to do. On the right, check them off when you have done them.

☆ Check off

1/

2/

3/

4/

5/

6/

7/

8/

9/

10/

11/

12/

13/

14/

What I want to see and do on my trip

Get a book or a magazine or other information about where you will be going. These will tell you a lot of things you will find interesting. You can also write to a Chamber of Commerce (an adult can help). Write below what you especially look forward to seeing or doing on your trip:

1/

2/

3/

4/

5/

6/

7/

8/

9/

10/

11/

12/

13/

☆Important information to write down and take along

My name

Home Address

City   State   Zip

My Telephone: Area code (   ) Number

Height   Weight   Age   Religion

The name of the adult I am with and where we will stay:

In case of emergency, please contact at home:

Name:

Telephone: (Area Code   )

My doctor or clinic:

Telephone: (Area Code   )

My special medical needs:

Special instructions in case of emergency

People I want to send postcards to

Name

Address

City   State   Zip

Name

Address

City   State   Zip

Name

Address

City   State   Zip

Name

Address

City   State   Zip

Name

Address

City   State   Zip

What I want to take along

You'll be gone for a while on your trip. You can help your adult decide on what you need to take with you. You will want to take a few things along to read and to play with. Write these below.

1/ _____
2/ _____
3/ _____
4/ _____
5/ _____
6/ _____
7/ _____
8/ _____
9/ _____
10/ _____
11/ _____
12/ _____
13/ _____
14/ _____

Special notes for my trip:

Here you can make a few notes to yourself. Perhaps you will want to remind yourself to pack a special game, or a special toy. Or, when you get to your vacation place, to send notes home to friends.

_____

_____

_____

_____

_____

_____

_____

_____

_____

_____

_____

_____

Part Two

☆ **On the road**

☆ **How to use your daily diary**

☆ **28 days of travel diary fun**

☆ **Extra games to play**

☆ **Puzzles**

☆ How to use your daily diary

Y ou can jot something down for each day of your trip. It's fun and it helps you keep a wonderful record.

Your diary devotes two pages to each day of your trip. You will find these **Today's Diary** pages on the next pages. There are enough diary pages for you to use each day for up to 28 days. Of course, if one day gets to be so much fun and you have so much going on you want to write about, you can use **more pages.** Here is where you can record the interesting things you see and do, as well as keep track of the things you eat and buy. Each day has a specially selected Fun Game for you to play. Let's look at these sections one at a time:

☆ Top of the page.

Date: July 7, 1992 Our weather is: Sunny!
Today we are in: Orlando, Florida

Here you jot some the basic diary facts of your day, such as the date, what the weather is like, and where you are. You don't have to be fancy about the weather, just say something like "sunny" or "it rained all day".

☆ What we did today:

This is your place to write down some of the things you did today that you most want to remember. Like this:

> ☆ What we did today: *We spent the entire day at Disneyland! What fun!*

Just some of the important things will do—it's not difficult, and shouldn't take more than a few minutes. Your journey and your experiences should give you good inspiration. Have fun!

☆ Things I liked best:

Think of what was the most fun or interested you the most. Write that down here.

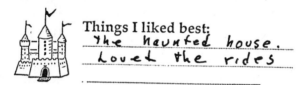

Things I liked best: *the haunted house. Loved the rides*

☆ What I saw or heard today that was funny:

Perhaps something funny happened to you or someone with you. Or you saw something that you felt good about. Jot this down.

What I saw or heard that was funny: *the spooks in the haunted house*

Some foods I ate:

Here you can tell some of the favorite things you ate or drank today. Be certain to write down if you tried anything new, and especially liked it.

Some foods I ate:
Hamburgers, Hot Dogs.
Really Pigged out!

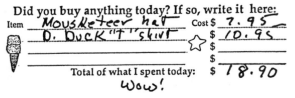 # Did you buy anything today?

Write down some of the things you bought today. Maybe you picked out a postcard to send to a friend or a relative. Or brought a small souvenir. Write these down as well as the price.

Did you buy anything today? If so, write it here:

Item		Cost
Mousketeer hat		$ _7.95_
D. Duck "T" shirt		$ _10.95_
		$ _____
		$ _____
Total of what I spent today:		$ _18.90_

Wow!

At the end of the day, you can add up what you spend. This is important, especially if you have only a certain amount of money to spend. Perhaps your adult will give you a small allowance of your very own to spend and to record.

Draw something you saw today:

Here's your chance to draw a picture of something you want to record in your book. It will be fun looking back someday at what you drew as a memory of this trip. At the bottom, don't forget to write a few words explaining a little about your picture.

Here's an example of a picture to draw. (Perhaps you can color this one.)

My picture is about:

☆ Fun Games:

Each day, you'll find a new fun game for you and your travel companions to play. There are more games in the back of the book.

Rapping with Rhymes

Here's your chance to do some mini "raps" with words you see along the way, such as on billboard or other signs. For example, if you see a sign that says, "Stop Ahead," you can use it in a rhyming rap that goes, "If you don't...Stop Ahead—You can get...a bop on the head." Everybody can take turns, or players can be chosen to rap with signs that everyone sees. (And if you don't...see any signs—you're just not going to have...any good times.)

Remember: Just jotting down a few words and facts each day can help you get more out of your trip or vacation. When your trip is over, your *Kid's Vacation Diary* will be filled with your personal observations and details. It will be a wonderful book for you to keep on your bookshelf to look at in the years ahead and to share with a friends—as well as a memory book your parents will treasure for years. ☆

 # Today's

Date: **Our weather is:**

Today we are in:

☆What we did today:

Things I liked best:

What I saw or heard that was funny:

Some foods I ate:

Did you buy anything today? If so, write it here:

Item	Cost $
	$
	$
	$

Total of what I spent today: **$**

Diary

Draw something you saw today:

[drawing box]

My picture is about: ‥‥‥‥‥‥‥‥‥‥‥‥‥‥‥‥‥‥‥‥‥‥‥‥‥‥‥‥‥‥‥‥‥‥‥‥‥‥

Today's Game: The Temple of Doom

As you travel along, the Temple of Doom lies somewhere ahead. You get caught in the Temple if you say the Forbidden Word, which you agree on in advance. It can be any ordinary word, in fact, the more ordinary the better. That's so you can trip up your players and send them to the Temple of Doom, where they have to remain silent for the next 5 miles or 5 minutes. Good words not to be spoken are "yes," "no," or perhaps, (toughest of all), "I." You can then start a general conversation about anything, but the persons who say the Forbidden Word are banished to the Temple of Doom. To vary the game, after a while, you can have several Forbidden Words.

Today's

Date: **Our weather is:**

Today we are in:

⭐ What we did today: ....
....
....
....
....

Things I liked best:
....
....
....

What I saw or heard
that was funny: ....
....
....

Some foods I ate:
....
....
....

Did you buy anything today? If so, write it here:

Item .... Cost $ ....
.... $ ....
.... $ ....
.... $ ....
         Total of what I spent today: $

Diary

Draw something you saw today:

My picture is about: ....
....

I Packed My Bag (wow!)

You've probably never packed a bag like this before where you are
limited only by your imagination. Name an object to pack, then say,
"I packed my bag, and in it I have a tank (or whatever you decide).
Then the next player says, "I packed my bag and in it I have a tank
and a plank (or whatever she or he decides to add). By the time the
game really gets going, you'll all have quite a bag. The objective is to
name everything in the bag, in sequence, or he or she is out. The winner is the last player who names everything correctly.

Today's

Date:

Our weather is:

Today we are in:

⭐ **What we did today:** ....

....

....

....

....

Things I liked best:

....

....

What I saw or heard that was funny: ....

....

....

Some foods I ate:

....

....

....

Did you buy anything today? If so, write it here:

Item .... Cost $ ....

.... $ ....

.... $ ....

.... $ ....

Total of what I spent today: $

Diary

Draw something you saw today:

My picture is about: ....
....

 True Colors

Pick a favorite color and then look for objects that are this color. For example, as you drive down the highway, you can say, "I see a red barn." Or, "I see a red car." The object is to see who can get the most objects of the chosen color in 15 minutes. Each player in turn can choose a different color. After you play this game for a while, you can make it a little harder by saying what you will count. For example, you could count only objects of a chosen color—which are not cars. Or trucks.

Today's

Date:

Our weather is:

Today we are in:

⭐ **What we did today:** ....

....

....

....

....

Things I liked best:

....

....

....

What I saw or heard
that was funny: ....

....

....

Some foods I ate:

....

....

....

Did you buy anything today? If so, write it here:

Item .... Cost $ ....

.... $ ....

.... $ ....

.... $ ....

Total of what I spent today: $ ....

Diary

Draw something you saw today: ☆ ☆ ☆

(empty drawing box)

My picture is about: ....

 ## The Tale Tellers

Everyone loves a good story, especially if he or she doesn't know where it will end. In Tale Teller, someone **starts a story**—one that he or she makes up or one that is already known. At an exciting place, the moderator calls, "Halt!" Then the **next person** continues telling the story—**his or her way, and with some variations.** Sometimes, the story really gets switched around! At another exciting place, "Halt!" is called—then another tale teller takes over. Sometimes, the next tale teller will go on with his or her own story by saying, "meanwhile, back at the ranch." The story goes on for as long as tale tellers tell tales. And you know how long that is.

☆

Today's

Date:

Today we are in:

Our weather is:

What we did today: ....

....

....

....

....

Things I liked best:

....

....

What I saw or heard
that was funny: ....

....

....

Some foods I ate:

....

....

....

Did you buy anything today? If so, write it here:

Item		Cost $
....		$ ....
....		$ ....
....		$ ....
....		$ ....
Total of what I spent today:		$

Diary

Draw something you saw today:

My picture is about: ....

 TV Game Show

All right, now you're on television. One of you is the game-show Moderator; the rest are guest panelists. The moderator picks a thing or an object (no people or ideas, please) and announces only that it's animal, mineral or vegetable. Then the panelists each in turn ask one question, such as, "is it bigger than a bread box?" The moderator can only say, yes or no. The panel has only 21 questions to use up; otherwise the game is over. Whoever wins is the next Moderator.

Today's

Date: Our weather is:

Today we are in:

⭐ What we did today:

Things I liked best:

What I saw or heard that was funny:

Some foods I ate:

Did you buy anything today? If so, write it here:

Item .... Cost $ ....

$ ....

$ ....

$ ....

Total of what I spent today: $

Diary

Draw something you saw today:

My picture is about: _____

_____

 The State Game

The leader gets to name a state and the others have to figure out what the last letter is of that state, and then name another state that begins with the last letter. For example if the leader calls, Minnesota, then the last letter is an A. So the game is to think of states that begin with A. (Hint: Alaska or Alabama, to name just two). The winner gets to name another state, and the game begins all over again. A variation is to play with the names of well-known countries (France, Japan, etc.) or world-famous cities (Paris, London), instead of state names.

 # Today's

Date: Our weather is:

Today we are in:

⭐ ## What we did today: ....

....

....

....

....

Things I liked best:

....

....

What I saw or heard
that was funny: ....

....

....

Some foods I ate:

....

....

....

Did you buy anything today? If so, write it here:

Item .... Cost $ ....

.... $ ....

.... ⭐ $ ....

.... $ ....

.... $ _____

Total of what I spent today: $

Diary

Draw something you saw today:

My picture is about: ....

....

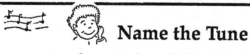 **Name the Tune**

Now you get a chance to be a little musical (or a lot). One player names a category, such as "blue" songs (Blue Moon, for example) or a word, and the others by turn get to name that tune. Some suggestions: songs that are about dances, favorite films or TV shows, travel, people's names, seasons, times of the day (such as sunset or night), or about romance. For a variation, the winner (or the loser) gets to sing them. Or everybody sings them.

Today's

Date: **Our weather is:**

Today we are in:

⭐ **What we did today:** ....

....

....

....

....

Things I liked best:

....

....

What I saw or heard that was funny: ....

....

....

Some foods I ate:

....

....

....

Did you buy anything today? If so, write it here:

Item .... Cost $ ....

.... $ ....

.... $ ....

.... $ ....

Total of what I spent today: $

Diary

Draw something you saw today:

My picture is about: ....

 Mindreaders

The moderator announces he or she has a famous person in mind—living or dead, but must be famous enough for everyone to recognize. The moderator says only the **first initial** of the **last name**. Then the "mindreaders" have to guess the name of the famous person by asking questions, beginning with, "Are you concentrating on ____?" The questions can only be by category, such as, "Are you concentrating on a famous actress?" "a rock star?" "a historical figure?" "Still alive?" "A woman?" And so on, until the famous person whose name begins with the letter is "mindread."

Today's

Date: Our weather is:

Today we are in:

⭐ **What we did today:** ....
....
....
....
....

Things I liked best:
....
....

What I saw or heard
that was funny: ....
....
....

Some foods I ate:
....
....
....

Did you buy anything today? If so, write it here:

Item ....   Cost $ ....
.... $ ....
.... $ ....
.... $ ....

Total of what I spent today: $

Diary

Draw something you saw today: ☆ ☆ ☆

My picture is about: ....

....

Scramble Up

Take a blank piece of paper and on it **scramble** a word so that it is not recognizable. For example, you can scramble the word, travel, by changing the letters around to make it read "velart," which is travel scrambled up. The game is for the rest of the players to figure out what the word is and put the letters in correct order on their piece of paper. Great fun. It's only fair that the best unscrambler gets to be the next scrambler.

Today's

Date:

Our weather is:

Today we are in:

☆What we did today:

....

....

....

....

....

Things I liked best:

....

....

What I saw or heard that was funny:

....

....

Some foods I ate:

....

....

....

Did you buy anything today? If so, write it here:

Item .... Cost $ ....

.... $ ....

.... $ ....

.... $ ....

Total of what I spent today: $

Diary

Draw something you saw today:

My picture is about: ....

....

I see

The first player looks about, perhaps out of the window of the car, then gives one clue, such as, "I see something red." Then the others have to guess what he or she sees. Each has one guess. The winner gets to be in charge of the next round of "I see."

Today's

Date: Our weather is:

Today we are in:

What we did today: ....
....
....
....
....

Things I liked best:
....
....

What I saw or heard
that was funny: ....
....
....

Some foods I ate:
....
....
....

Did you buy anything today? If so, write it here:

Item .... Cost $ ....

.... $ ....

.... $ ....

.... $ _____

Total of what I spent today: $

Diary

Draw something you saw today:

My picture is about: ....

....

Crazy Pictures

Take a sheet of paper and fold it in thirds. On the top third, the first player draws the head and neck of a person, animal or thing, unknown to the others. When he or she is finished, the page is folded over so that just the bottom of the picture shows. The next player draws the body on the second third of the page. Or course, second player should not know what the first player was drawing. The third player gets to finish the bottom third of the sheet by drawing the legs and the feet. Unfold sheet—and there you have a crazy picture! Perhaps you can even think of a fun name for your creation.

Today's

Date:

Today we are in:

Our weather is:

What we did today: ....
....
....
....
....

Things I liked best:
....
....

What I saw or heard
that was funny: ....
....
....

Some foods I ate:
....
....
....

Did you buy anything today? If so, write it here:

Item .... Cost $ ....
.... $ ....
.... $ ....
.... $ ....

Total of what I spent today: $

Diary

Draw something you saw today:

[blank drawing box]

My picture is about: ....

....

⭐ The Hangman

Here's an ages-old game. The hangman thinks of a word, then on a sheet of paper, draws a **dash** for **each letter** of the word, then also draws a gallows. The player, or gallows bird, has to guess what the word is, one letter at a time. When the letter is correct, it is drawn over the dash; when the "bird" guesses wrong, the hangman draws in a figure on the gallows: first a head, then nose, mouth, eyes, ears, hair, body, hands, legs, and feet. In all, a "bird" can get hung in 10 bad guesses. The last thing to be drawn, of course, is the noose. Words to be guessed can range from simple, short words to more complex titles of songs.

Today's

Date:

Our weather is:

Today we are in:

⭐ What we did today: ....

....

....

....

....

Things I liked best:

....

....

What I saw or heard that was funny: ....

....

....

Some foods I ate:

....

....

....

Did you buy anything today? If so, write it here:

Item .... Cost $ ....

$ ....

⭐ $ ....

$ ....

Total of what I spent today: $

Diary

Draw something you saw today:

My picture is about: _____

_____

I Spy!

All the players become "spies," on the lookout for something they agree upon in advance. That can be most anything; for example, if the game players are in a car, that can be a red barn. Everyone tries to locate a red barn; the first to see one cries, "I spy!" He or she gets one point; if two say "I spy" at the same time, each get one point. Whoever gets to 10 points first wins and gets to pick the next object. Objects can be a bridge, a red car, a yellow sign, a horse, or even a car with a certain license plate, such as a Texas plate.

Today's

Date: **Our weather is:**

Today we are in:

⭐ **What we did today:** ....

....

....

....

....

Things I liked best:

....

....

What I saw or heard
that was funny: ....

....

....

Some foods I ate:

....

....

....

Did you buy anything today? If so, write it here:

Item .... Cost $ ....

.... $ ....

.... $ ....

.... $ _____

Total of what I spent today: $

Diary

Draw something you saw today:

My picture is about: ....

....

Signs O The Times

Look for signs as you drive along and try to get words you see beginning with **alphabetical letters** in order. The first person to see an "A"
on a word on a sign calls out "A"; then the next person tries to find a
word beginning with a "B," and so on. Letters must be in order. The
person who sees the most letters from A to Z wins. But be warned:
You'll really have to look hard for some letters, like X and Z.

Today's

Date:

Today we are in:

Our weather is:

☆ What we did today: ....

....

....

....

....

Things I liked best:

....

....

What I saw or heard that was funny: ....

....

....

Some foods I ate:

....

....

....

Did you buy anything today? If so, write it here:

Item	Cost $
....	$ ....
....	$ ....
....	$ ....
....	$ _____

Total of what I spent today: $

Diary

Draw something you saw today:

My picture is about: ....

....

Rapping with Rhymes

Here's your chance to do some mini "raps" with words you see along the way, such as on billboard or other signs. For example, if you see a sign that says, "Stop Ahead," you can use it in a rhyming rap that goes, "If you don't...Stop Ahead—You can get...a bop on the head." Everybody can take turns, or players can be chosen to rap with signs that everyone sees. (And if you don't...see any signs—you're just not going to have...any good times.)

Today's

Date: Our weather is:

Today we are in:

 What we did today: ....

....

....

....

....

Things I liked best:

....

....

What I saw or heard
that was funny: ....

....

....

Some foods I ate:

....

....

....

Did you buy anything today? If so, write it here:

Item ....   Cost $ ....

.... $ ....

.... $ ....

.... $ ....

Total of what I spent today: $

Diary

Draw something you saw today:

My picture is about: ....
....

Famous Me

Here's everybody's chance to be a **star** or a celebrity. One person is **Famous Me**—a person well known in history, television, motion pictures or sports. The players ask the "celebrity" questions trying to find out his or her identity, but the famous person can only answer with a yes or a no. (Or a nod or shake of the head). The limit is 16 questions. Whoever guesses right can be the famous person next. Wow!

 # Today's

Date:

Today we are in:

Our weather is:

What we did today: ....

....

....

....

....

Things I liked best:

....

....

What I saw or heard
that was funny: ....

....

....

Some foods I ate:

....

....

....

Did you buy anything today? If so, write it here:

Item .... Cost $ ....

.... $ ....

.... $ ....

.... $ _____

Total of what I spent today: $

Diary

Draw something you saw today:

[Empty drawing box]

My picture is about: ....

What's Happening?

One person carefully acts out an every day deed—in **pantomime**. For example, the person may be watching a ping pong game (with head going back and forth) or brushing teeth or even driving a car. The players each take turns guessing what's happening. The winner gets to be the next one to perform a pantomime.

 # Today's

Date: **Our weather is:**

Today we are in:

What we did today: ....
....
....
....
....

Things I liked best:
....
....

What I saw or heard that was funny: ....
....
....

Some foods I ate:
....
....
....

Did you buy anything today? If so, write it here:

Item .... Cost $ ....
.... $ ....
.... $ ....
.... $ ....

Total of what I spent today: $ _____

Diary

Draw something you saw today:

My picture is about: ··
···

Follow Me

Everyone follows the leader's activity—then adds one activity of his or her own. For example, the game can be started by the leader holding his or her nose. The next person has to follow this example by holding his or her nose, then adding some activity, such as sneezing. The next person, in turn, holds his or her nose, sneezes, then adds something (like snapping fingers.) The game goes on with each player adding one more thing, after exactly repeating what went on before. The player who misses a thing is out. The winner is the player who stays in the longest.

 # Today's

Date: Our weather is:

Today we are in:

⭐ What we did today: ....

....

....

....

Things I liked best:

....

....

What I saw or heard
that was funny: ....

....

....

Some foods I ate:

....

....

....

Did you buy anything today? If so, write it here:

Item .... Cost $ ....

.... $ ....

.... ⭐ $ ....

.... $ _____

Total of what I spent today: $

Diary

Draw something you saw today: ☆ ☆ ☆

My picture is about: ....

Charades

One person will make up a charade, and the rest will try to guess. The subject can be the name of a TV show, a movie, book, or a song title. The player holds up his or her fingers to indicate **number** of words. Then, he or she holds up a finger to indicate first word, second word, so on, while performing a charade. Everyone tries to guess what's going on—and the winner is the person who correctly guesses the full name or title.

Today's

Date: Our weather is:
Today we are in:

 What we did today: ....

....

....

....

Things I liked best:

....

....

What I saw or heard that was funny: ....

....

....

Some foods I ate:

....

....

....

Did you buy anything today? If so, write it here:

Item .... Cost $ ....

.... $ ....

.... $ ....

.... $ ....

Total of what I spent today: $

Diary

Draw something you saw today:

My picture is about: ....
....

Eek! How Awful

Into a paper bag, secretly collect a few items, such as a grape, a sock, a feather, a paper clip, a coin—the more fun the better. Players in turn close their eyes, then insert their hand to feel and touch the objects and to describe them. Eek! How Awful. You'll be surprised how imaginative the answers you can get from ordinary, everyday things.

Today's

Date: Our weather is:

Today we are in:

☆ What we did today: ....

....

....

....

Things I liked best:

....

....

What I saw or heard
that was funny: ....

....

....

Some foods I ate:

....

....

....

Did you buy anything today? If so, write it here:

Item ....   Cost $ ....

.... $ ....

.... $ ....

.... $ ....

Total of what I spent today: $

Diary

Draw something you saw today: ☆ ☆ ☆

My picture is about: ....

....

Opposites

They say opposites attract, and in fact, one opposite will attract another in this game. Choose up sides so each person has an "opponent." In turn, each opponent says one word, and his or her opponent says the opposite of the word previously said. For example, one says no, the other yes; stormy, fair skies, and so on. Here's the catch: each has only 3 second to answer. The player giving the most answers in a certain time wins, or goes on to play other winners in a group.

Today's

Date: Our weather is:

Today we are in:

⭐ What we did today: ....

....

....

....

....

Things I liked best:

....

....

What I saw or heard
that was funny: ....

....

....

Some foods I ate:

....

....

....

Did you buy anything today? If so, write it here:

Item ....   Cost $ ....

.... $ ....

.... $ ....

.... $ ....

Total of what I spent today: $

Diary

Draw something you saw today: ☆ ☆ ☆

My picture is about: ....

....

Hotter—colder

Here the main player decides on an object within the car or room, and everyone tries to learn what it is. The main player will say **hotter** when the guesses are in the right direction; **colder** when they are going the wrong way. Winner gets to be the main player.

Today's

Date:

Our weather is:

Today we are in:

What we did today:

....

....

....

....

Things I liked best:

....

....

What I saw or heard that was funny:

....

....

Some foods I ate:

....

....

....

Did you buy anything today? If so, write it here:

Item	Cost $
....	$ ....
....	$ ....
....	$ ....
....	$ ....

Total of what I spent today: $

Diary

Draw something you saw today:

My picture is about: ....

....

Duplicating Machines

One person is chosen as It, who begins the game by making some motion, such as rubbing his or her nose. Then It points to another player, who, in turn, has to duplicate what It has done and add one more motion of his or her own. This player, in turn, points to another player who has to duplicate all that has gone on before—plus add one more. Winner is the person who duplicates all without getting anything out of sequence.

Today's

Date: Our weather is:

Today we are in:

What we did today: ....
....
....
....
....

Things I liked best:
....
....

What I saw or heard that was funny: ....
....
....

Some foods I ate:
....
....
....

Did you buy anything today? If so, write it here:

Item ....   Cost $ ....

.... $ ....

.... $ ....

.... $ ....

Total of what I spent today: $

Diary

Draw something you saw today: ☆ ☆ ☆

My picture is about: ....

☆ Simon Says

Here's a fun game that's a lot more complicated than it sounds. One player is "Simon," and only he or she gives the orders. The object of the game is to only follow those orders specifically preceded by the words, "Simon Says." For example, if Simon says, "sit up!" and a person sits up, then that person is out of the game. However, if *Simon says: "Simon says, 'sit up,'"* that's a correct order. After a few easy drills, once Simon starts giving orders quickly, then one by one players will drop out. Some example of orders: Hold out your hands...hands up! Simon says, hands up. Turn around...look right. Of course, Simon has to say it first for it to be a proper command. Winner gets to be Simon.

Today's

Date: Our weather is:

Today we are in:

What we did today:

....

....

....

....

....

Things I liked best:

....

....

What I saw or heard that was funny:

....

....

....

Some foods I ate:

....

....

....

Did you buy anything today? If so, write it here:

Item ....   Cost $ ....

.... $ ....

.... $ ....

.... $ ....

Total of what I spent today: $

Diary

Draw something you saw today: ☆ ☆ ☆

My picture is about: ....

The Awful Cat

Here's a word game to see how many, and often ridiculous ways, you can describe that Awful Cat. Beginning with the A letter, the first person says, "The neighbor's cat is an awful cat." The next person repeats, but has to think up another way to describe the cat, beginning with the letter A, such as atrocious, athletic, arty, or even artificial cat. When a round has been completed, go on to the next letter of the alphabet, B, (bedeviled, bald, etc) and so on. If the player doesn't think of a word within 15 seconds, she or he can only yowl or meow when his or her turn comes next. Winner is the last one remaining to describe that awful cat.

Today's

Date: Our weather is:

Today we are in:

What we did today: ....

....

....

....

....

Things I liked best:

....

....

What I saw or heard that was funny: ....

....

....

Some foods I ate:

....

....

....

Did you buy anything today? If so, write it here:

Item .... Cost $ ....

.... $ ....

.... $ ....

.... $ ....

Total of what I spent today: $

Diary

Draw something you saw today: ☆ ☆ ☆

My picture is about: ....

☆ Mirror Image ☆

One person is chosen to be the mirror, and the rest of the players mirror him or her for two minutes. The idea is that each player must be an exact mirror image of the mirror—often with very funny results (some people are cracked mirrors). Here are some basic things the group might try to mirror image: stick out a tongue, laugh heartily, cross eyes, wink one eye at a time, meow piteously, pretend to drive a car or fly an airplane.

Today's

Date: Our weather is:

Today we are in:

⭐ **What we did today:** ....

....

....

....

....

Things I liked best:

....

....

What I saw or heard
that was funny: ....

....

....

Some foods I ate:

....

....

....

Did you buy anything today? If so, write it here:

Item ....   Cost $ ....

.... $ ....

.... $ ....

.... $ ....

Total of what I spent today: $

Diary

Draw something you saw today:

My picture is about: ....

Jolly Green Giant

As we all know, the Jolly Green Giant goes "Ho, Ho." In this game, the first player says, "ho." The second player says, "ho, ho." And so on around the ring of players, each adding a ho-hoing in his or her own way, in the right number, and each adding a ho! With a little imagination, the ho-hoing can be hilarious. The object is that anyone can laugh—except the person ho-hoing. That person must be very quiet, or else he or she is eliminated from the game. The one who has the most staying power, and remembers the right number of ho-hoes, is the winner.

Today's

Date: Our weather is:

Today we are in:

What we did today: ....

....

....

....

....

Things I liked best:

....

....

What I saw or heard
that was funny: ....

....

....

Some foods I ate:

....

....

....

Did you buy anything today? If so, write it here:

Item .... Cost $ ....

.... $ ....

.... $ ....

.... $ ....

Total of what I spent today: $

Diary

Draw something you saw today:

My picture is about: _____

 Contact!

While you're in the family car, traveling along, try this game of coordination. The idea here is for the players (except for the driver, of course!) to **choose an object** that you can see not too far ahead, such as a historical marker, a famous landmark, or even a car in the opposite lane. All players close their eyes, and when each thinks the chosen object is exactly alongside, he or she hollers, **"contact,"** then opens his or her eyes. Winner is the person who guesses correctly or is closest. An alternative to this group game is for each player in turn to play contact.

Extra Games
to Play

Going on a Sailing Trip

You're going sailing for a long time, and of course, you have to take things along with you. Trouble is, you can only take along things beginning with the letter *S*. So can your crew. You begin by saying, "I'm going on a sailing trip and I'm taking along a snake." Your other players also have to repeat what you said, then add one thing of their own. This also must begin with an S. Those who forget the sequence, or can't think of something to take along beginning with an S, are out. Winner is the last person still going. (Then, you can start the game all over again with a *new* letter).

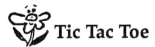 ## Tic Tac Toe

On a piece of paper, draw two lines up and down and two lines sideways. Each player in turn gets to place a mark of an X or an O in each small square. The player that first gets three marks in row wins. Rows must be vertical, diagonal or horizonal lines. Like this:

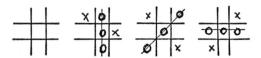

You can also play a variation by making the same four lines, but then closing the ends into a box. Instead of playing the boxes, you play your X and O's on the intersections. Like this. You need three in a row to win, once again.

GAMES AHEAD

Alphabet Game

U CAN PLAY

As you go down the road, or look around a place, you can play the Alphabet Game. Look for signs that have letters. Begin looking for the letter A. The first person to see an A gets 1 point. Write that down. Then, look for the letter, B, and so on. You need to go in alphabetical order. The first person to name the letter gets the point. The player with the most points wins.

A/   N/
B/   O/
C/   P/
D/   Q/
E/   R/
F/   S/
G/   T/
H/   U/
I/   V/
J/   W/
K/   X/
L/   Y/
M/   Z/

Popeye

This is a game you can play at night. Look for a car with just one headlight, the "Popeye." The first person to see this yells, "Popeye," and then gets to slap or punch the person next to him or her on the shoulder. (But not too hard, please!)

The Color Purple

The main player picks something inside the car, train or plane (however you're traveling) which is a certain color, such as purple. He or she then says, "Color me purple," and in turn, others try to guess what object he or she has chosen. If a couple of rounds don't locate the specific item, then players can ask specific questions as to its size or location. Winner gets to pick the next color and object.

Blind artist

Get a sheet of paper and a pencil. Blindfold whoever is "it," and then place the tip of the pencil on the paper. The blindfolded person is then told what to draw—an airplane, a car or a ship. The fun comes as everyone sees what the blind artist draws. Take turns.

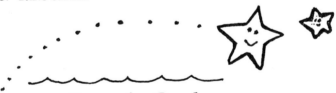

Cross the Creek

Here's a game for inside your motel or hotel room. Get some pieces of paper (maybe a newspaper) and one person lays pieces in an irregular line, but only stepping distance apart. These are stepping stones. Each person has to step carefully, or he or she will end up in the creek. The rules are that only ONE FOOT can be on a "stone" at a time. For an added variation, certain really smart persons can also balance a book on their heads. If they step off the "stone," or lose their book, they fall in the creek—and are out.

Lucky Pennies
Two games with pennies*

First game:

You will need 10 pennies per player. Taking turns, each player secretly puts a number of pennies in his or her closed hand. The object of the game is to take turns guessing how many pennies the player has in hand. Winner gets the pennies. But if the guessers do not name the correct amount in the hand, they lose from their penny hoard the amount the player had in hand. Hint: Play with just a few pennies at first.

Second game:

A longer-lasting variation: You can play this game with just one opponent. The player again secretly places from one to ten pennies in his or her closed hand, then places the hand in front of the opponent. The opponent must guess odd or even amounts of pennies. If he or she is right, the opponent wins a penny. If he or she is incorrect, the opponent loses a penny. The game goes on until no pennies are left to play with, or, after a certain amount of time has gone by, the winner is the one with the most pennies.

*Note: You can also play this game with toothpicks or other small objects.

What are these pictures trying to tell us?
The answer is at bottom of the page

Charade Pictures

You play this game by drawing pictures, instead of acting out a charade. The first player chooses a topic, as in charades. She or he can choose from a title of a popular kid's book, a well-known song, or a hit movie. Also, the player can choose a funny or contemporary saying, or the title or something from a famous nursery rhyme. The fun part is that he or she can't use any words.

On a piece of paper, he or she draws pictures representing the charade on paper. The opposing players try to guess the subject. The person who guesses the topic the quickest is the winner and gets one point. Then, it's time to change, and the winner has a turn to be the main player.

You also can divide into teams, if you like, and decide jointly how you want to present your subject.

The boy at left has his hands up by his ears, as if they were large, and is gently making a mooing noise. He is trying to represent a cow. In the center picture, the boy is jumping up (see his feet?). In the last picture, we see a moon. What is the Picture Charade? If you guessed, The Cow Jumped Over the Moon, you were 100 percent right.

Guess the Charade Picture

Here are some charade pictures for you to guess (or to use in your games). The answers are at the bottom of the page.

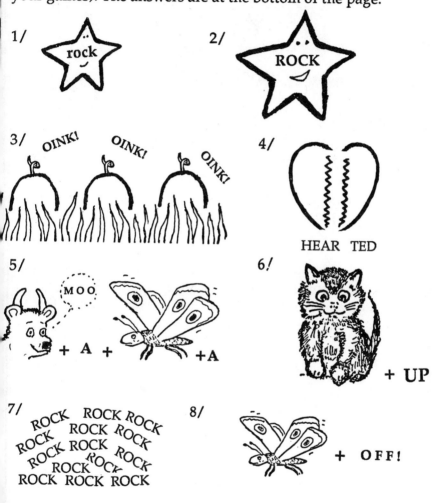

1/ rock

2/ ROCK

3/ OINK! OINK! OINK!

4/ HEAR TED

5/ MOO + A + +A

6/ - + UP

7/ ROCK ROCK ROCK ROCK ROCK ROCK ROCK ROCK ROCK ROCK ROCK ROCK ROCK ROCK ROCK ROCK

8/ + OFF!

Charade Picture Answers: 1/ Rock star 2/ Big rock star 3/ Three Little Pigs (tails-up in tall grass) 4/ Broken hearted 5/ Cowabunga 6/ Catsup 7/ A pile or rocks or a rock pile 8/ Bug off (as in, "get out of here!")

Fencing Kids

It's sort of like a mini-fencing match, in which you and your opponent can make thrusts with your trusty pencil. You can fence sideways, and up and down, between the dots. You can't move diagonally. Each player gets one move at a time to connect two dots. Then, it's the other player's turn. Your goal is to complete a square to put your initial in it. Then you get another turn. If you see someone else closing a square, you can *block* their move by putting in your line, when your turn comes. And, of course, you have to be careful not to get caught connecting the third side of a box when your turn comes, because then your opponent then can close the box to claim the point. The champion kid fencer is the one with the most squares.

Round 1/   Round 2/

· · · · ·   · · · · ·

· · · · ·   · · · · ·

· · · · ·   · · · · ·

· · · · ·   · · · · ·

· · · · ·   · · · · ·

Round 3/

Round 4/

Round 5/

Round 6/

Round 7/

Round 8/

Round 9/   Round 10/

Round 11/   Round 12/

Round 13/   Round 14/

87

Round 15/

Round 16/

Round 17/

Round 18/

Round 19/

Round 20/

Circle Games

Try to find the words spelled out below. Each circle contains just one word. Your job is to figure out the word. You must find the starting letter and then read clockwise (the way a clock turns). You can't skip a letter. For example, in the circle game above, the starting letter is C. Reading clockwise, you will find that the word is "CAR." (Don't peek now, but the answers are on the bottom of the page, upside down)

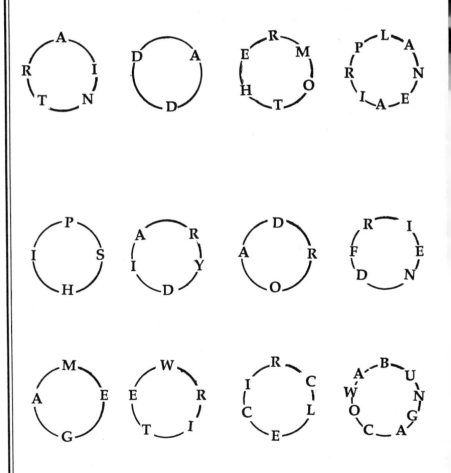

Word Games:

Rapid Riddles

1/ What do you have that others use more than you? 2/ What smells the most in the house? 3/ It falls down all the time, but never gets hurt. What is it? 4/ You give this away all the time, but still you can keep it. What is it? 5/ What kind of coat can you put on wet and still be happy with? 6/ What is black and white. but read all over? 7/ What's very light but you can't hold for long? 8/ What is faster—hot or cold? 9/ What word do you always pronounce wrong? 10/ Even when the world seems gloomy, where can you always find happiness?

Silly States—Do You Live in Nooger?

Oh, my! Someone has misspelled the following states—and you have to be a detective and put them back in order. For example, "Sotaminne," isn't a soft drink. It's the state of Minnesota, all scrambled up. Here are some more states for you to unscramble:

1/ Sinconwis   6/ Ippssimissm
2/ Sexta   7/ Driflao
3/ Enw orky   8/ Sillioni
4/ Ouths Kotada   9/ Enaim
5/ Noogeɪ   10/ Doahi

Answers (printed upside-down):

Silly States Answers: 1/ Wisconsin 2/ Texas 3/ New York 4/ South Dakota 5/ Oregon 6/ Mississippi 7/ Florida 8/ Illinois 9/ Maine 10/ Idaho

Rapid Riddles Answers: 1/ Your name 2/ Your nose 3/ Rain 4/ Your word 5/ Coat of paint 6/ A newspaper 7/ Your breath 8/ Hot, because you can catch cold 9/ The word, wrong 10/ In your dictionary.

Car ☆ games

Try to identify each of the following. Write your initials if you are the first to see each item. The winner is the one who has seen the most subjects the first.

___Car with open trunk ___Car with hood up ___Car with trailer hitch ___Car with door open ___Car the same kind and color as your own ___Car with spare tire carried on rear end ___Convertible car (with or without top down) ___Station Wagon ___Volkswagen "beetle"___Car with luggage on top

☆ Colorfully yours

Try to find things that are of the following colors. The first to see these writes it down, and, puts his or her initials after each, to indicate he or she is the one who saw it first:

1/ White

2/ Black

3/ Blue

4/ Red

5/ Yellow

6/ Green

7/ Orange

8/ Pink

☆ ☆ ☆

Part Three

Memories

⭐ My final thoughts about this trip

⭐ Names, addresses & places to remember

⭐ Things I saved from my trip

My final thoughts about this trip

Here, you can sum up some of your vacation or trip experiences. For example, did you have a good time overall? Did you have some "worst moments?" Would you change anything the next time you travel? And, lastly, you can "rate" your trip on a scale of 1 to 10. Make 10 the very best; 1 the worst ever.

My final comments:

I especially remember these good times:

My worst moments:

What I'd do differently the next time I travel:

On a scale of 1 (worst) to 10 (best), I'd rate this trip:

The end!

Names, addresses & places to remember

Travel is an adventure. You will be making new friends as you travel as well as seeing interesting places. Here, you can write down names and addresses, so that later you can keep in touch with them.

1/ Name _____ Age ___ Phone ___
Address _____
City _____ State ___ Zip ___

2/ Name _____ Age ___ Phone ___
Address _____
City _____ State ___ Zip ___

3/ Name _____ Age ___ Phone ___
Address _____
City _____ State ___ Zip ___

4/ Name _____ Age ___ Phone ___
Address _____
City _____ State ___ Zip ___

5/ Name _____ Age ___ Phone ___
Address _____
City _____ State ___ Zip ___

6/ Name _____ Age ___ Phone ___
Address _____
City _____ State ___ Zip ___

7/ Name _____ Age ___ Phone ___
Address _____
City _____ State ___ Zip ___

Special memories:

Things I saved
from my trip

Here you can keep small personal mementoes of your vacation. You can be creative (so long as everything fits, of course). Some souvenirs you might want to keep here are ticket stubs to a favorite place or fun ride, a picture postcard or two that you picked out, printed materials you saved from places you visited, some foreign currency samples, if you went abroad, or even a favorite photograph or two. Under each item, you can write a few words that will help you remember, such as the date, where you were, what it was like, or where you got the item.

Special memories: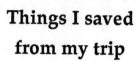

Things I saved
from my trip